A Day in the Life of a...

Teacher

Carol Watson

FRANKLIN WAT
NEW YORK•LONDON•SYDN

Sonia Harvey is an infant school teacher.
At 7.30 a.m. she arrives at school and starts preparing the classroom for the day ahead.

At 8.50 a.m. Mrs Harvey asks the school children to line up in the playground.

Mrs Harvey greets her class and shows the children into the school.

"Time for the register, Year 1," says Mrs Harvey. The children sit together quietly and read their books until their names are called out.

Next Mrs Harvey takes Year 1 to join the rest of the school in the hall for assembly. "There are five birthdays today," says Mrs Westwood, the teacher in charge.

Mrs Harvey plays the piano as everyone sings.

After assembly, Mrs Harvey sets up weighing and measuring activities for some of Year 1. "How many cubes have you used, Melissa?" she asks.

Then Mrs Harvey helps the other children with their project work.

She helps Olivia on the computer. "What information can we find here?" Mrs Harvey asks.

At 10.30 a.m. it's playtime.
Mrs Harvey is on 'playground duty'.
She has a drink of coffee while she
watches over the children.

8

After play Year 1
have their drinks, too.

"Who wants a biscuit?"
Mrs Harvey asks.

Next Mrs Harvey
listens to her
class reading.
"Can you tell me
that word, Anand?"
she asks.

Meanwhile Mrs Mott, a helper, does an art activity with some of the children.
"Make sure you stick the hair on properly, Elliot," she says.

At 12.00 it's lunch time.
Mrs Harvey has a snack and chats with
the other teachers in the staff room.

During the break Mrs Harvey has a singing class with the older children.

Then Mrs Harvey teaches the recorder group. "We'll learn a new tune, today," she tells them.

13

At 1.30 p.m. Mrs Harvey returns to her own class. There, she helps some children with a water activity and tells others how to look after Toffee, the guinea pig.

During the afternoon break
Mrs Harvey has a meeting with
Mr Jones, the headteacher.
"We need to talk about the school
concert," he says.

At the end of the afternoon, Mrs Harvey
gathers the children together for a story.
"And what do you think the
wise owl said?" she asks.

Now it's home time. Mrs Harvey tells the children to wait for their parents to collect them.

Mrs Harvey talks to one of the mums. "Michelle has done some good work, today," she says.

When everyone has gone home, Mrs Harvey tidies the classroom, does some marking, and pins the masks that the children made on the wall.

Get your sketchbooks from here

Get your maths books from here

Now it's 5.30 p.m. and she sets off for home. "This has been a really busy day," Mrs Harvey says to herself.

Test your friends

Your teacher tests you to see what you have learnt. You can test yourself and your friends.

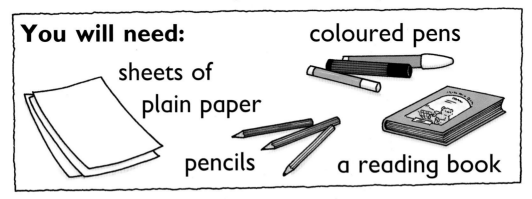

You will need: coloured pens

sheets of plain paper

pencils a reading book

1. Look in your reading book and choose some words to write on your paper. Find words that are easy to spell and others that are harder.

2. Write five words on each sheet of paper. (You could put words into 'word families' like the ones below):

mat	hen	dip	hop
cat	men	rip	top
sat	ten	lip	mop
fat	Ben	sip	pop

3. Ask an adult to check that the words are correct before you start.

4. Get into pairs. Ask your partner to write down the words on your list. Then you do the same with their list.

5. Now play teacher. Mark each other's work. Swap over lists and see how many your friend has got right. Put a coloured tick next to the correct words.

How you can help your teacher

1. Be helpful and kind to other children and teachers.

2. Look after school things carefully.

3. Make sure your clothing is always marked with your name.

4. Always tell your teacher if you are worried about something.

5. Listen carefully when your teacher talks to your class.

6. Make sure you come to school on time.

Facts about teachers

There are different kinds of school teacher - Infant, Junior and Secondary. Sonia is an Infant teacher. She works at a Primary school. Her class is Year 1. Primary schools are divided into two sections - Infant and Junior. The children are grouped according to age.

Infant school
- Nursery class   3-4 years
- Reception class   5 years   Key Stage 1
- Year 1/middle infants   6 years
- Year 2   7 years

Junior school
- Year 3/ first year junior   8 years
- Year 4/ second year junior 9 years   Key Stage 2
- Year 5/ third year junior   10 years
- Year 6/ fourth year junior   11 years

Secondary school
This is for children aged 12-18

To be a teacher you need to like children, be good at explaining things and have a good sense of humour.
You also need to be enthusiastic, organized and very patient.

Index

© 1998 Franklin Watts

Franklin Watts
96 Leonard Street
London
EC2A 4RH

Franklin Watts Australia
14 Mars Road
Lane Cove
NSW 2066

ISBN: 0 7496 2970 3

Dewey Decimal Classification
Number: 371

10 9 8 7 6 5 4 3 2 1

A CIP catalogue record for
this book is available from the
British Library.

Printed in Malaysia

Editor: Samantha Armstrong
Designer: Kirstie Billingham
Photographer: Steve Shott
Illustrations: Kim Woolley

With thanks to: Sonia Harvey,
Adjoa Ezekwe, Gwynne Jones
and all the staff and children of
Grove Park Primary School,
Chiswick, London.

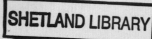